INFP PERSONALITY - DISCOVER YOUR GIFTS AND THRIVE AS THE IDEALIST PRINCE OR PRINCESS

THE ULTIMATE GUIDE TO THE INFP PERSONALITY TYPE INCLUDING: INFP CAREERS, INFP PERSONALITY TRAITS, INFP RELATIONSHIPS, AND FAMOUS INFPS

FIND HEALTH, WEALTH, AND HAPPINESS AS AN INFP.

DAN JOHNSTON

Published by Dan Johnston

www.DreamsAroundTheWorld.com

CONTENTS

WHY YOU SHOULD READ THIS BOOK

You know those people for whom everything just seems so easy?

Their career or business is always getting better. Their relationships appear happy and fulfilling. They have a satisfying home life, work life, and, by damn, never seem to have a complaint in the world. **Let's call these people the "Thrivers."**

Then there are those for whom life feels like a constant upward swim. At work, they feel like they don't belong. Their relationships are either problematic or unsatisfying. To them, life has always been a struggle. Let's call them the Strugglers.

What's going on here? Are some of us just blessed with good fortune? Is everyone else just cursed with constant struggle?

Don't worry, there are no magical forces at work - just some psychology. It's been my experience that there is only one difference between the Strugglers and the Thrivers.

The Thrivers, by reflection, study, or just dumb luck, have built their lives around their natural personalities. Their work utilizes their strengths while their relationships complement their weaknesses.

A small percentage of the Thrivers came into their lives "naturally." The careers their parents or teachers recommended were the perfect fit for them, or they had a gut feeling that turned out to be right. They met their ideal partner who complemented them perfectly. I believe, however, that this group is the minority.

Most Thrivers have spent years "watching" themselves and reflecting about who they really are. For some, this is a natural process. For others (myself included), it's a more deliberate process. We read, studied, questioned, and took tests all in the name of self-awareness. We've made it a priority to know and understand ourselves.

Whatever a Thriver learns about themselves, they use to make significant changes in their lives. They change careers, end relationships, and start new hobbies. They do all this so that one day their lives will be fulfilled and will have a natural flow: a life in which they can thrive.

This book is for Thrivers: past, present, and future.

If you once had your flow but can't seem to find it again, read on.

If you're in your flow and want to keep and improve it, read on.

And if you're one of the beautiful souls struggling but committed to finding your flow and to thrive, you're in the right place. Read on.

Today you may feel like a salmon swimming upstream, but this is a temporary state. One day soon, you will find yourself evolving. Perhaps into a dolphin, swimming among those with whom you belong, free to be yourself, to play, and to enjoy life. Maybe you'd rather find your place as a whale - wise and powerful, roaming the oceans and setting your own path, respected and admired by all.

KNOWLEDGE BRINGS AWARENESS AND AWARENESS BRINGS SUCCESS

I'm an entrepreneur as well as a writer. As an entrepreneur, negotiation plays a big part in any success I might have. One of the secrets to being a good negotiator is always to be the one in the room with the most information.

The same holds true for decision making in our personal lives. When it comes to the big things in life, we can't make a good decision if we don't have all the relevant information.

I think most of us understand this on an external level. When we're shopping for a new car, we research our options: the prices, the engines, and the warranties. We find out as much as we can to help make our decision.

Unfortunately, we often forget the most important factor in our decisions: Us.

A Ford Focus is a better economic decision and a more enjoyable drive than an SUV...but that doesn't matter if you're seven feet tall or have five kids who need to be driven to hockey in the snow.

When it comes to life decisions, such as our work or relationships, who we are is the most important decision factor.

It doesn't matter if all your friends say he is the perfect guy; it only matters if he's perfect for you. It doesn't matter if your family wants you to be a lawyer, a doctor, or an accountant.... What do you want to do? If you make your decision based on what the outside world says, you won't find the levels of happiness or fulfillment you desire.

IF YOU MAKE YOUR DECISION BASED ON WHAT THE OUTSIDE WORLD SAYS, YOU WON'T FIND THE LEVELS OF HAPPINESS OR FULFILLMENT YOU DESIRE.

In order to make the best decisions for you, you must first know yourself. That is the purpose of this book: to provide the most in-depth information on your personality type, the INFP, available anywhere.

By reading this book you will:

- Improve self-awareness.
- Uncover your natural strengths.
- Understand your weaknesses.
- Discover new career opportunities.
- Learn how to have better relationships.
- Develop a greater understanding of your family, partner, and friends.
- Have the knowledge to build your ideal life around your natural personality.
- Have more happiness, health, love, money, and all around life success while feeling more focused and fulfilled.

FREE READER-ONLY EXCLUSIVES: WORKBOOK AND BONUSES

When I wrote this book, I set out to create the most *useful* guide available. I know there will always be bigger or more detailed textbooks out there, but how many of them are actually helpful?

To help you get the most from this book, I have created a collection of free extras to support you along the way. To download these, simply visit the special section of my website: www.PersonalityTypesTraining.com/thrive

You will be asked to enter your email address so I can send you the "Thriving Bonus Pack." You'll receive:

1. A 5-part mini-course (delivered via email) with tips on how to optimize your life so you can maximize your strengths and thrive.
2. A compatibility chart showing how you are most likely to relate to the other 15 personality types. You'll discover which people are likely to become good friends (or better) and whom you should avoid at all cost.
3. A PDF workbook to ramp up the results you'll get from this book. It's formatted to be printed, so you can fill in your answers to the exercises in each chapter as you go.

To download the Thriving Bonus Pack, visit:

www.PersonalityTypesTraining.com/thrive

DISCLAIMER

I know this book will serve you well in discovering your strengths and building your self-awareness. I have researched and written this book based on years of practical experience including running multiple businesses, talking to dozens of people about their strengths and weaknesses, and applying this knowledge to my own life to discover my strengths and build a business around what I do best. With that said, I must emphasize that I am not a psychologist, psychiatrist, or counselor, or in any way qualified to offer medical advice. The information in this book is intended to improve your life but it does not replace professional advice in any way, nor is it legal, medical, or psychiatric advice. So, if you're in a bad place or may be suffering from a mental illness, please seek professional help!

INTRODUCTION TO THIS SERIES

The goal of this series is to provide a clear window into the strengths, weaknesses, opportunities, and challenges of each type.

You'll discover new things about yourself and find new ways to tap into your strengths and create a life where you thrive. I want you to have every advantage possible in the areas of work, play, relationships, health, and finance.

This book is part of a series; each one focuses on one "type." You will find that I write directly to you, although I do not make an assumption as to your personality type or your traits. I will generally refer to the type, aka INFP, instead of saying "you." Not every trait of a specific type applies to everyone of that type, and we never want to make any assumptions about who you are or about your limitations.

I would recommend beginning with your type to learn most about yourself, but don't stop there. Each book focuses on a particular type and will be valuable for that type, but will be equally valuable for family, friends, bosses, and colleagues of that type.

Even before writing these books, I found myself doing extensive reading on the types of my brother, parents, friends, and even dates. In my business, I would research the types of my assistants, employees, and potential business partners. I found that learning about myself got me 60% of the way, and the other 40% came from learning about the other people in my life.

If you plan to read up on all the different types, I suggest looking at my "Collection" books, which include multiple types all in one book for a reduced price. It'll be easier and a better price for you than buying each individual book.

You'll find a link to all the other books in this series at the end of this book.

ADVICE FROM INFPS FOR INFPS

After publishing the first edition of this book, I reached out to a group of INFPs. I asked them what advice they would share with a younger, perhaps less experienced INFP, that would help them live the best life possible.

I thought I would include them in this updated edition, and what better way to kick things off?

You can learn a lot about a type by what they say, and also by how they say it. So, allow me to present a few of their inspiring and mostly unedited answers here. You'll find the rest towards the end of the book.

"Love God and do what you want!"

"Don't be afraid. Go for it. Even the blows will prove beneficial in the end."

"Don't live your life afraid of being hurt. Your heart is too big, learn who to give to. Embrace change, let it make you strong. Don't apologize for your feelings, be thankful for them. The world needs us."

"Look after your health."

"The world doesn't owe you anything, but you owe everything to the world."

"No matter where you are in life, never give up on searching on your true self because everyone sees life as a game where there are losers and winners, but always remember that life is not a game but a wonderful journey...."

"Try to achieve happiness, or whatever it means to you, the rest is just detail. Then again I haven't really lived enough to have the right to give advice, so taking this could be a bit... iffy...."

"Happiness starts from within. Things will fall into place when you establish inner harmony; you won't find peace because of things falling into place."

"Love yourself, but never stop improving."

"Look in the mirror and smile, because, as long as you have yourself, you have the best friend anyone could ever ask for and you'll never be alone."

"Simple. Just believe you can do it."

"Take up all the opportunities presented to you, you won't lose anything, just go for it and enjoy yourself!"

"If I could give one piece of advice to a younger INFP and only one piece of advice, it would be this: Learn fiscal responsibility at as young an age as you possibly can, because when you follow your dreams, it will be utterly vital to have financial discipline, because the things INFPs love to do don't pay well, but that doesn't mean you can't do them; it just means you have to be smarter with money than office drones."

"You might try to please everyone at once. Just don't forget you should be the first in the list."

"Be yourself.

Trust your instinct.

Accept the inevitable change.

Don't put others on a pedestal.

Feel the moment, don't bottle them up.

Grow, adapt, and overcome.

Love with every part of your being.

Have no regrets.

Enjoy your childhood and its lack of responsibilities.

Care for yourself and your well-being more than others. They can take more than you can give if you let them."

"Save as much as you spend.... Let yourself love as much as you can.... You are unique and it is wonderful, by accepting that a weight should be lifted off your shoulders, you are not alone, do something funny or stupid each day, experience as much as you can."

This section of the book will always be growing. If you're an "experienced" INFP and you'd like to add your insight, wisdom, and advice to upcoming editions, you can email me at: me@thedanjohnston.com .

INTRODUCTION TO MYERS-BRIGGS®

I first officially discovered personality psychology about five years ago. I say officially because I do have some vague memories of taking a career test in high school that was likely based on the Myers-Briggs® instrument, but who really pays attention to tests when you are 16?

The Myers-Briggs assessment is one of many options in the world of personality profiles and testing. It is arguably the most popular, and in my opinion it is the best place to start. I say this because the results provide insight into all aspects of our lives, whereas other tests are often focused on just career.

The Myers-Briggs instrument is based on the idea that people are quite different from one another. These differences go deeper than emotions, moods, or environment, and speak to how we're actually wired to behave.

And, as it turns out, most people end up being wired 1 of 16 ways, based on four groups of characteristics.

This doesn't mean we can't build certain traits or change our behavior. Rather, knowing your personality type is an opportunity to learn which traits come most naturally to you and which areas you may find challenging or need to invest time in developing.

Your type provides a platform to understand yourself and create a plan for personal growth based on your unique personality strengths and weaknesses.

It is also an opportunity to understand the people around you and get to the root of many conflicts. In fact, you may find that understanding the different types and how others relate to you is the most valuable aspect of the Myers-Briggs instrument.

THE 16 TYPES AND 4 GROUPS

In total there are 16 different personality types that are described by a unique series of 4 letters.

At first, the types appear confusing, but they're really quite simple.

Each type is based on one of two modes of being or thinking for each of the four letters.

E (extrovert) or I (introvert)

N (intuitive) or S (sensing)

T (thinking) or F (feeling)

P (perceiving) or J (judging)

Now, don't pay too much attention to the words tied to each letter because they don't actually offer a great description for the characteristic.

In just a second, I'll share my explanation for each letter. But just before this, I want to share an important point to remember: Personality analysis and profiling is a bit of an art, as well as a science. In other words, since people are so diverse, the descriptions and results aren't always black and white. Some people have a strong preference for one mode or the other, but others are closer to the middle. It's natural for all of us occasionally to feel or demonstrate traits of the other types.

What we want to focus on here is your natural way of being and the functions you are strongest in. It is also important to know that you can, and will, develop your secondary (or auxiliary) and third (or tertiary) "functions" over time and with practice. In doing so, you will create a more balanced personality with fewer weak spots and a more diverse set of skills. In fact, the key to overcoming most personality challenges is to develop your weaker functions.

Generally, it's said that we grow our primary (or dominant) function in our early years, our secondary function in our twenties and thirties, and our third function some time in our thirties and forties. However, this assumes you're not being proactive nor are reading a book like this one. In your case, there is no reason you can't leap ahead a few decades and strengthen your other functions ahead of schedule.

WHAT THE FOUR LETTERS MEAN

As you know, there are four letters that make up your personality type.

At first, these letters can be a little confusing, especially since their descriptions aren't the most telling.

Here's how I explain each letter.

For the first letter in your type, you are either an E or an I.

The E or I describes how you relate with other people and social situations.

Extroverts are drawn to people, groups, and new social situations. They are generally comfortable at parties and in large groups.

Introverts are more reserved. This is not to say that introverts do not enjoy people, they do. Introverts are just happier in smaller groups, and with people they know and trust like friends or family. Keep in mind, this does not mean that introverts are not capable of mastering social skills if they must. Rather, they will not be drawn to such situations or find the process as exciting or enjoyable as an extrovert would.

"The Deal Breaker": For some people E or I is obvious. For

others, the line is blurred. This question will make your preference clear: "Does being around new people or groups add to or drain your energy? If you spent an entire day alone would you feel "off" or bad, or would you be just fine?" If you can spend a day or two alone without feeling bad, or if spending a few hours in a group of people leaves you feeling tired, well then you're an introvert.

While extroverts may often steal a lot of the attention in a room, introverts often have the upper hand. While many extroverts crave the spotlight, introverts are able to sit back and calmly observe, learning more about a situation and making their contributions more meaningful and impactful.

Further, introverts have the ability to work alone for long periods. In many professions, such as writing, this is a significant advantage.

INFPs are introverts. This is why INFPs are so capable at working alone, are self-sufficient, and usually not interested in building large social groups.

For the second letter, you are either an N or an S.

This trait describes how you interact with the world.

Those with the intuitive trait (N) tend to be introspective and imaginative. They enjoy theoretical discussions and "big picture" kind of ideas. For an extreme example, imagine a philosophy professor with a stained suit jacket and a terribly messy office.

Of course, this isn't the reality for most N's. Most intuitive people live a happy, fulfilled life full of new ideas and inspirations...all while managing the day-to-day aspects of their lives at an acceptable level. N's, and especially INFPs, have an exceptional imagination and ability to form new ideas, tell stories, and inspire those around them.

Those with the sensor trait are observant and in touch with their immediate environment. They prefer practical, "hands on" information to theory. They prefer facts over ideas. For an extreme example, think of a mechanic or military strategist.

INFPs have the intuitive trait. This is why they are drawn to ideas and have such a strong imagination.

Third, you are either a T or an F.

This trait describes how you make decisions and come to conclusions, as well as what role emotions play in your personality and how you deal with them.

Those with the thinker trait are "tough-minded." They tend to be objective and impersonal with others. This can make them appear uncaring, but they are generally very fair. Those with the thinking trait rely on logic and rational arguments for their decisions. The "T" trait would be common among (successful) investors and those who need to make impersonal and objective decisions in their careers.

Those with the feeler trait are personal, friendly, and sympathetic to others. Their decisions are often influenced by their emotions or the "people" part of a situation. They are also more sensitive and impacted by their emotions, and less afraid to show their emotions to the outside world. The "F" trait would be common among counselors and psychologists.

INFPs have the feeling trait. The foundation of the INFP personality is their intuitive and thinking traits. This makes them idealistic, optimistic, sympathetic, and capable of great deeds.

Lastly, you are either a P or a J.

This trait describes how you organize information in your internal and external worlds. This translates into how you schedule yourself, stay organized, and evaluate your options.

Perceivers are best described as "Probers" or "Explorers." They look for options, opportunities, and alternatives. This means they tend to be more creative, open minded, and, well, often have messy bedrooms. They're happy to give one plan a try without having all the details beforehand, knowing they can adjust or try something else in the future.

Judgers are structured and organized. They tend to be more consistent and scheduled. Spreadsheets may be their friends and their rooms will be clean...or at least organized. They prefer concrete plans and closure over openness and possibilities.

You would find more P's among artists and creative groups, whereas professions like accountants and engineers would be almost exclusively J's.

INFPs have the perceiving trait. This feeds their creativity and adaptability. It is why they have such great imaginations, are able to come up with new ideas, and are happy proceeding with a plan before all the details are worked out.

THE FOUR GROUPS

Since the original creation of the 16 types, psychologists have recognized four distinct groups, each containing four types. The four types within each group have distinct traits in common based on sharing two of the four traits.

- The four types are:
- The Artisans (The SPs)
- The Guardians (The SJs)
- The Idealists (The NFs)
- The Rationals (The NTs)

As an INFP, you are an Idealist.

Idealists are abstract and compassionate. Seeking meaning and significance, they are concerned with personal growth and finding their unique identity. Their greatest strength is diplomacy. They excel at clarifying, individualizing, unifying, and inspiring. The two roles are as follows:

Mentors are the directive (proactive) Idealists. Their most developed intelligence operation is developing. The attentive counselors and the expressive teachers are the two role variants.

Advocates are the informative (reactive) Idealists. Their most developed intelligence operation is mediating. The attentive healers and the expressive champions are the two role variants.

The other three Idealist types are:

- The Champions: ENFPs
- The Leaders: ENFJs
- The Protectors: INFJs

To learn more about how all the types relate and interact, download the free compatibility chart at:

www.PersonalityTypesTraining.com/thrive

DISCOVERING THE "HEALER" AND "PRINCESS": WHO IS AN INFP?

At this point, I'm going to assume you're an INFP and are reading about yourself, or reading about someone you care about who is an INFP.

I'm also going to assume you've read some of the basic descriptions online about INFPs and have bought this book because you want depth and details on how INFPs can thrive.

So I'm not going to bore you with a lengthy or redundant description of an INFP. Rather, you will find a concise description here, followed by more details and specifics in the following chapters on strengths, weaknesses, careers, and relationships.

INFPs are meditative and introspective, cooperative and accommodating, informative and enlightening, attentive and thoughtful.

Their peaceful exterior masks an imaginative and passionate inner world.

INFPs are reserved, private individuals. As children, INFPs are often misunderstood, particularly in practical families who have trouble understanding their passion and idealism. Most types can shrug off mix-matched parental expectations, but INFPs often have trouble here. They want their parents to be happy and this often leads them to put forth one front to their parents, hiding parts of themselves, while keeping another part inside. This can be troublesome, because INFPs seek unity of mind, body, and spirit.

INFPs have a strong sense of right and wrong and an idealistic way of looking at the world. They care deeply about causes and issues they've connected with, and will devote themselves to the cause when necessary. These causes are usually connected with people or animals, as INFPs are highly empathetic and believe in the rights of others as much as their own.

INFPs are flexible, patient with complex situations, and comfortable with new ideas and information. On the other hand, INFPs cringe at routine work, repetitive tasks, and boring details.

An INFP's idealism, empathy, and strong system of values are not common traits within society and, being only about one percent of the population, it's easy for INFPs to feel isolated in their way of thinking. This can be especially tough because INFPs value harmony and acceptance. It's important for every INFP to remember that these differences that can make them feel so isolated are actually some of their greatest strengths and a gift to the world.

SOME COMMON TRAITS FOR INFPS

- Reserved
- Moral
- Value driven
- Idealistic
- Self-sufficient
- Independent
- Flexible
- Creative
- Imaginative
- Caring
- Empathetic

- Harmonious
- Courageous
- Loyal, Devoted
- Future-oriented, optimistic
- Inspirational
- Authentic
- Sensitive
- Complex
- Growth-oriented

IN GOOD COMPANY: FAMOUS INFPS

As an INFP, you are among some very good company. In this chapter, you'll find a collection of famous and "successful" people who are either confirmed, or suspected, as being INFPs.

Do not use this chapter as a guide to what you must do, or whom you must resemble. Rather, use this chapter as a source of inspiration. It is a chance to see what's possible as an INFP and what great things have been accomplished by those who share a similar makeup to you.

Personally, I have found great value in studying famous people from my own type, including reading their autobiographies. Most of us spend the early years of our lives feeling lost and trying to figure out our purpose or how we want to end up. I've found studying those of my type who have found their purpose, and then success, gives me a shortcut to understanding my own potential and the directions my life could go.

FAMOUS INFPS

Writers, Creators, and Thought Leaders

- George Orwell
- J.R.R. Tolkien (Author of 'The Lord of the Rings')
- C.S. Lewis
- Virginia Woolf
- Antoine de Saint-Exupery (Author of 'The Little Prince')
- Jean-Jacques Rousseau
- Soeren Kierkegaard
- Albert Camus

- A.A. Milne (Author of 'Winnie the Pooh')
- Bill Watterson (Cartoonist famous for 'Calvin & Hobbes')
- J.K. Rowling (Author of the 'Harry Potter' series)
- Franz Kafka
- Edgar Allan Poe
- John Milton
- William Blake
- William Shakespeare
- Vincent van Gogh
- Augustine
- Hans Christian Andersen (Author of 'The Emperor's New Clothes' and 'The Ugly Duckling')
- Homer (Author of 'The Iliad' and 'The Odyssey')

Actors and Performers

- Louis C.K.
- Jude Law
- Robert Pattinson
- Andrew Garfield
- Mary-Kate Olsen
- Chloe Sevigny
- Terrence Malick
- David Lynch
- Andy Warhol
- Teller
- David Simon (Creator of The Wire)
- Bjork
- Fiona Apple
- Thom Yorke
- Morrissey
- Johnny Depp

- Tim Burton
- Heath Ledger
- Kurt Cobain
- Nicolas Cage
- John Lennon
- Jim Morrison

Politicians

- John Kerry

Worth Noting: If you haven't yet read up on any of the other types, you may not notice the distinctions of the famous INFPs. Compared with other types, INFPs have a strong tendency to avoid business and politics. They excel in creative fields.

Considering INFPs are only about 1% of the population, it is incredible how many of our favorite fantasy worlds and characters were created within the mind of an INFP. INFPs have created hundreds of imaginative worlds, including: Lord of the Rings, Harry Potter, Winnie the Pooh, and Calvin and Hobbes.

On a more somber note, the INFPs who find fame often struggle with staying happy or remaining grounded. The rate of debt, drug use, and depression among famous INFP actors and performers is higher than with most other types.

Both these patterns come back to the same central theme: INFPs have a powerful imagination and a tendency to lose themselves in their own thoughts. This gives the INFP incredible imaginative abilities, but also makes it easy for them to slip into a "dark place." *It's important for an INFP to monitor their thoughts and find outlets to express themselves with people who understand them.*

GOING DEEPER EXERCISE

Of the famous INFPs on this list, which are most familiar to you?

_____

_____

_____

_____

_____

What are some common elements you notice? These could be specific personality traits or characteristics. It could also include actions they have taken or tough decisions they have made. For example: going against the grain or choosing to follow a passion.

_____

_____

_____

_____

_____

YOUR SECRET WEAPONS

(Aka your unique strengths)

In my own life, I have found no greater success secret than discovering, *and applying*, my strengths.

When we are young, we are often taught that we need to be good at many things. For example, success in school is based on your average grade. Most parents would much prefer their child have a smooth report card of all B+s than one with two A+s and two C-s.

The real world doesn't reward the well-rounded individual, at least not exceptionally well. Those who receive the greatest rewards are those who focus on their strengths and ignore all else. Think of people like Arnold Schwarzenegger, Steve Jobs, and Oprah Winfrey.

Does anyone *really* care if Oprah is bad at math, if Arnold has trouble managing his personal life, or if Steve Jobs was a bit of an ass to employees from time to time?

Nope. No one cares because each of these Greats focused on their strengths and created an extraordinary life for themselves.

Oprah (an ENFJ) harnessed her empathy and ability to build trust and bond with people to create incredible interviews and connect with her audience.

Arnold (an INTJ) used his focus, discipline, and strategic thinking to achieve incredible goals in fitness, performing, and politics, despite being the underdog in almost everything he ever did.

Steve Jobs (an ISTP) kept his energy focused on his creative and visual strengths. His visions were so clear, and his innovations so impressive, that his social graces didn't matter.

33

Now, as you read on, you will discover the unique strengths closely linked to INFPs. While you read this, remember that these are the strengths that come naturally to you, but you still need to develop and fine-tune them if you want to thrive.

AN INFP'S SECRET WEAPONS

INFPs are:

- Growth and future oriented. This means INFPs look for new possibilities and find ways to improve themselves along the way.
- Warm and kind to other people. They will generally put others before themselves and prefer to be of service to others when possible.
- Loyal and genuinely interested in other people and can be very perceptive. They will naturally strive for win-win solutions.
- Great communicators who are able to express themselves, their ideas, and their visions exceptionally well.
- Able to develop deep connections with others and have a strong capacity for love and caring.
- Tied to a strong value system and will remain true to what they believe is right. Being grounded in their values can give them incredible energy and persistence when working towards a goal or championing a cause.

Extremely accepting of other people and their differences. INFPs see people as equal and tend to believe in everyone's potential. This adds to the INFP's gift to develop and inspire people. They will often see the potential in another person, even when that person doesn't see it in themselves. This can be applied to team building, recruiting, managing, and leadership (not to mention parenting).

Very creative and have the best imagination of any type. This imagination, combined with their forward thinking, gives them the ability to inspire others through their ideas and visions for the future.

INFPs will benefit when they apply their creativity to create new products, or use their imagination to create new worlds for stories, movies, or art.

- Bright and intelligent, INFPs can generally keep up with those around them and have no problem grasping new or complex ideas.
- Very adaptive and can function well in many situations. They're very comfortable with change and do well in stimulating or uncertain situations that require adaptability and quick thinking.
- Passionate. When connected with an issue or individual, an INFP can become very vocal and determined. This makes INFPs particularly powerful advocates for causes, whether that of a forward thinking company, a charity, or a social movement.

In summary, a developed INFP can be:

- Intelligent
- Adaptable
- Creative
- Insightful
- Imaginative
- Well-liked

- Caring
- Intuitive
- Authentic
- Supportive
- Inspiring
- Innovative

KEYS TO USING YOUR STRENGTHS AS AN INFP

1. Give yourself plenty of alone time to develop your ideas and let your imagination flourish. Don't feel pressured to please everyone by giving them your time. Make yourself a priority and schedule this recharging alone time.

 2. Avoid being the "finisher" on projects. Your gifts are in the creation and early phases of a project. Focus on this and leave the details to other people.

3. Align yourself with people and work that share your value system. When you work for a company you believe in you'll feel alive and inspired, and have a never-ending source of energy. If you take a job for a paycheck, you'll feel drained and conflicted.

4. The same goes for who you spend time with. You have a great moral compass and internal value system. Don't ignore it or silence it in the presence of others who don't align with your values.

In this and future chapters, you will discover "Going Deeper" exercises. These are designed to help you better understand and apply the chapter's content. If you're like me, you may want to write down your answers. When you bought this book you also got access to a companion workbook you can print and then fill in with your answers as you go. You can download the workbook for free at:

www.PersonalityTypesTraining.com/thrive

GOING DEEPER EXERCISE

Of the strengths listed above, which most jump out at you as strengths of your own?

_____

_____

_____

_____

_____

What are three strengths listed above that you know you have but are not actively using in your life, at least not as much as you know you should?

_____

_____

_____

_____

_____

How could you apply these strengths more frequently?

_____

_____

_____

_____

_____

YOUR KRYPTONITE

(Aka your potential weaknesses)

You didn't think I was going to stop at your strengths, did you? As much as I say *focus on your strengths,* it is still important to be aware of your weaknesses, even if it is just so you can ignore them more easily.

Below, you will find a list of weaknesses and challenges common among INFPs. As with strengths, this is not a definitive list and do not take it as a prescription for how INFPs have to be.

Sometimes I will see posts in a Facebook group for a specific type where people seem overly proud of their type challenges. I remember one post on an ENFP group making light of how the poster had been unable to tidy their room in four days. While it was good for a "we've all been there" chuckle, I did find myself turned off when I thought about what a chaotic life this person must have. They have chosen to neither fix their weakness (by developing their self-discipline and follow through) nor embrace them (by hiring a maid). Instead, they have chosen to suffer what they described as four days of agony simply trying to clean a room.

So, if some of these weaknesses don't really resonate with you, that's **good**. Ignore them and don't assume you should be weak in that area, if you're not. If you do connect with some of the weaknesses, take it as an opportunity to either work to improve that area of yourself, or to accept the weakness and find a solution so you don't have to deal with it.

✓ INFPs' challenges tend to revolve around confrontation, judging people (including themselves) too harshly, and following through with the details of life. INFPs will find life easier and more fun if they learn to perceive themselves and the world

39

around them objectively.

COMMON KRYPTONITE FOR THE INFP

- The INFPs' powerful imagination and tendency to take responsibility for whatever happens can lead them to "dark" thoughts.

- INFPs may not give themselves enough credit when it's due. They can be too hard on themselves when things aren't perfect.

- INFPs do not like to be controlled or to control others. This isn't a negative trait, but it can lead to problems with their superiors, or as a superior themselves when their employees need more structure and direction.

- INFPs generally shy away from confrontation. This can lead to tension building and unresolved issues lingering in their relationships.

- INFPs are very sensitive to negative criticism even if it is meant to be constructive.

- INFPs are value driven, and at the same time can be perfectionists. This combination can lead to blaming themselves for whatever goes wrong...while judging the outcome by very strict and impossible to meet standards or values. INFPs aren't alone in this combination. It's common for all the Idealist types, but INFPs tend to put themselves through the most pain via their judgments.

- INFPs' dislike of confrontation and conflict makes it hard for them to end bad relationships or leave work that isn't right for them.

- INFPs are often shy or reserved and have difficulty opening up and expressing their feelings with people (especially those they don't know well). At the same time, they can be easily offended. This combination makes it very hard for those around them who may feel like they're always walking on thin ice, unsure what they can and can't say around the INFP.

✓ INFPs may react too emotionally to stressful or difficult situations. Once under stress, they may be unable to understand other points of view and become oblivious to how their behavior affects others.

OVERCOMING YOUR WEAKNESSES

Most challenges INFPs face come from the relationship between their values and beliefs, and their way of perceiving the world (both how it is and how it should be).

Because they are so sensitive to criticism, INFPs are prone to developing an internal viewpoint of the world...and then blocking out any information that runs contrary to it.

✓ It is common for INFPs to perceive only what they want to perceive and "look for" information that backs up their existing viewpoints while blocking out everything else. This way of thinking leads the INFP to appear selfish and unrealistic, and can lead them to isolating themselves further.

The key to success for INFPs is developing their Extroverted Intuition. This allows INFPs to more objectively and accurately perceive the world around them. This means becoming comfortable with disagreement and learning to understand other points of view.

Make an effort to read more autobiographies. Take time to really listen to, and understand, other people. Make a habit of engaging people in debate and genuinely try to take a perspective different from your own. This will help you become more open

41

minded and learn to turn off the filter on incoming information.

When taking in new information, pay attention to your process. Are you sincerely concerned with the truth, or are you just looking for information that supports what you already believe?

GOING DEEPER EXERCISE

Of the weaknesses listed above, which three do you most recognize in yourself?

_____

_____

_____

_____

_____

What are three weaknesses listed above that you know are having a significant negative impact on your success?

_____

_____

_____

_____

_____

How could you reduce the impact these weaknesses have on your life, either by learning to overcome them or eliminating the activities that bring them to the surface?

_____

_____

_____

_____

_____

IDEAL CAREER OPTIONS FOR AN INFP

If you gave a Myers-Briggs test to a group of a few hundred people from the same profession, you would see a very clear pattern.

An accountant in my martial arts class told me that of 600 chartered accountants who took the Myers-Briggs test at his firm, he was one of only three people who didn't score the same type.

This happens for two reasons:

1) Selection Bias: People with the personality type for accounting will tend to do well in related tasks and receive hints that that kind of work is right for them. They may especially enjoy numbers, spreadsheets, etc.

2) Survival Bias: Those with the personality type for accounting are most likely to pass the vigorous tests and internships required to become a chartered accountant.

We are actually much better at finding the right path for us than we give ourselves credit for. In almost every profession, there is a significantly higher percentage of those "typed" to excel in it than random chance would have.

Yet, many people still slip through the cracks, or spend decades searching for that perfect career before finding it.

This chapter will help you avoid the cracks and stop wasting your precious time. Below, you'll find a comprehensive list of careers INFPs tend to be drawn to and succeed in.

There are many more career options beyond this list that I have seen in other books and have intentionally not included here. These include "good" options that an INFP could easily do and succeed in, but would not be as happy or fulfilled as they would in another profession where they could use their real strengths.

I have included only the options I believe INFPs have an upper hand in *and* the highest likelihood to find fulfillment and success. There are always other options, but why swim upstream if you don't need to, right?

To be most successful, an INFP should focus on work that:

- Allows them to follow their inspirations and create new products, ideas, or ways of doing things.
- Gives them autonomy and uninterrupted time alone to develop ideas.
- Is performed within a flexible structure.
- Doesn't involve frequent presentations or evaluations in front of groups.
- Rewards enthusiasm, imagination, original thought, and ideas.
- Is service focused and aligned with their personal beliefs and values. To an INFP, authenticity is very important and they must believe in the work they are doing.
- Happens within a friendly and supportive environment with a minimal amount of conflict.

POPULAR PROFESSIONS FOR INFPS

In Creative Fields

- Playwright ✓
- Writer ✓
- Poet ✓
- Novelist ✓
- Character actor ✓
- Desktop publisher
- Interior decorator
- Musician/composer ✓

- Artist
- Desktop publisher
- Art director
- Multimedia producer
- Cartoonist ✓
- Story teller/designer ✓
- Set designer

Education/Counseling/Religion

- College professor
- Researcher ✓
- Counselor ✓
- Social worker ✓
- Librarian ✓
- Educational consultant
- Special education teacher
- Bilingual education teacher
- Early childhood education teacher
- Employee assistance counselor
- Child welfare counselor
- Planned-giving officer
- Philanthropic consultant
- Career counselor/coach
- Grant coordinator
- Genealogist ✓
- Curator
- Public health educator

Health Care

- Dietitian/ nutritionist
- Home health social worker
- Occupational therapist
- Speech-language pathologist/ audiologist
- Holistic health practitioner
- Ethicist

Business / Technology / Organizational Development

- Employment development professional
- Human resources development professional
- Social scientist
- Diversity manager (human resources)
- Consultant on team building and conflict resolution
- Organizational psychologist
- Outplacement consultant
- Labor relations specialist
- Corporate team trainer
- Customer relations manager
- Staff advocate (technology consultant)
- Coach
- Human resources recruiter

GOING DEEPER EXERCISE

Read through the list above and answer the following questions:

Which 5-10 careers jump out at you as something you'd enjoy doing?

_____

_____

_____

_____

_____

Thinking back to the sections on strengths, what do you notice about the list of careers? What strengths might contribute to success in these careers?

_____

_____

_____

_____

_____

THRIVING AT WORK

There is an astronomical difference between a job you're good at and a career or pursuit in which you thrive.

While some people are fine just getting by, people like you and I sure aren't. This section will help you thrive at work.

THREE FOUNDATIONS FOR THRIVING AT WORK

1) Be aware of your strengths and weaknesses, and be selective of the work you do. Be honest in job interviews about where you excel as well as where you struggle.

2) When in a job, take this same honest approach with your supervisor. Explain that you aren't being lazy; rather you feel you could deliver much more *value* to the company by focusing on your strengths.

3) At least once per week, if not daily, stop for a few minutes and ask yourself if you're working in your strengths or struggling in your weaknesses. Remember, you have unique and valuable gifts...but make the effort to use them and avoid getting trapped in the wrong kind of work.

When it comes to your work, be sure to tap into these work related strengths for INFPs:

- The ability to think outside the box and find new possibilities. Applying this skill to creative fields can lead to new ideas and excellent results.
- The ability to work well alone when required. Don't underestimate the value of this strength. Many people can't function well alone, or waste hours every day with chitchat. Your ability to work alone means more productivity, and gives you an upper hand on your

competition.

- Thoughtfulness and the ability to "go deep" and study a subject in depth.
- Exceptional at one-on-one work. INFPs have an excellent ability to understand and communicate with people in an intimate setting. This is an excellent skill for HR people, managers, leaders, coaches, and therapists.
- INFPs can make an unstoppable commitment to work they believe in. This makes them excellent champions of important causes or forward thinking companies. When they apply this commitment to an important cause, INFPs are capable of changing the world.
- Ability to easily understand others. Can often "read between the lines" where others miss an unspoken point. This gives INFPs an upper hand in many forms of communication. It also allows INFPs to write incredible stories with lots of hidden meaning.
- Adaptability. INFPs are comfortable with change and the unknown, and they're able to quickly change direction or adapt their approach for better results. This is especially valuable in new or fast growing companies.
- INFPs are one of the types with an excellent ability to see the big picture. This allows them to better understand the consequences of certain actions or ideas before moving forward with them.
- INFPs have a natural curiosity and the ability to study and understand a subject quickly. This allows them, if they're interested in the topic, to jump into projects and quickly get up to speed. This is a valuable skill in fast moving or diverse work environments.

To maximize their success, INFPs should be aware of some challenges they face at work. INFPs will not always, but may:

- Be disorganized and have difficulty with scheduling, prioritizing tasks, or planning their work. This can contribute to indecisiveness about what to do next.

Hey, this comes with the territory, and is common among creative types. Fortunately, if an INFP focuses on their strengths, they will be valued by their company and have no problem getting support with organization.

- Be impatient with those who are less creative than them, or those who tend to "ponder" things before making a decision. This is natural, but can create conflict. INFPs should make an effort to understand and appreciate these other types, and utilize the "planners" to help them with organization and long-term planning.

- Lack the discipline to complete tasks or follow through on details. Sometimes this is OK, in the case when a better opportunity or use of time has come up. Other times it can be looking for an easier route. INFPs will benefit from taking the time to honestly reflect on their motivation for not following through on a task or commitment.

- Dislike rigid tasks, people, or systems. This isn't so much a weakness as a preference and should impact where an INFP looks for employment.

- Have trouble coping with interruptions, especially frequent ones like phone calls. This goes hand-in-hand with the INFP's ability to focus and go deep on an issue. This is another reason why a quiet and private workspace will greatly benefit an INFP. INFPs work best when they are given the time and space to think through ideas and apply themselves without pressure or interruptions.

- Bad at estimating how long things will take. Being

idealists, they tend to assume things will happen much quicker than they actually do. This can lead to making unrealistic goals from putting too much focus on what "could be possible" and then coming up short of their objectives.

- Easily become bored or sidetracked when the exciting part of a project ends, or when confronted by repetitive tasks. This is a tough one to get around, so it is best to avoid positions where these kinds of tasks are required.

- Dislike of criticism and conflict. This can lead to trouble receiving feedback from superiors, or giving it to subordinates. Learning to listen to and accept constructive criticism is an important area of improvement for INFPs.

RICH AND HAPPY RELATIONSHIPS

Whoever said opposites attract never met an ENFP + ISTJ couple.

Sure, you want a partner who complements your strengths and weaknesses, but most of us also want someone who understands us: someone to whom we can express our opinions and ideas and be understood.

In this section, we'll start with a discussion on what INFPs are like in relationships. Then we'll look at the most common personality types INFPs are happy with. Lastly, we will provide some advice on creating and maintaining successful relationships as an INFP and *with* an INFP.

INFPs In Relationships

INFPs initially appear to be calm and laid back partners. Inside, this isn't really the case. INFPs experience the world and their relationships with intense emotions.

Once they give their heart to someone, INFPs are intensely loyal, committed, and loving. In fact, INFPs are capable of the deepest levels of love, loyalty, and caring, but they won't give their heart to just anyone.

Because they experience emotions so intensely, and are generally very sensitive, INFPs begin their relationships closed off and reserved. This is an effective defense mechanism to save themselves from heartbreak. They must feel a lot of trust before they will let their guard down and open themselves up to another person.

INFPs' IDEAL MATCHES

Because INFPs can get lost in their own heads, and often have trouble "objectively" viewing a situation, they are well matched with more logical and stable types, such as ENTJs. This provides them with a "rock" and an anchor to help bring them back to reality when needed. It also means their partner is unlikely to be pulled into their emotional struggles and will be comfortable dealing with any difficult situations (confrontation, negotiation, etc.) on behalf of the couple.

A note on compatibility: There is no be all and end all. The information on type compatibility is either based on theory or surveys, neither of which will ever provide a universal rule.

For example, NF (Idealist) types find the greatest relationship *satisfaction* dating NFs. This is likely because they can share a common way of thinking and feeling about the world. Yet, according to Jung, the ideal partner for an INFP is an ENTJ. The two have complementary personalities and are perhaps most likely to be successful in a business partnership or in creating a home...but this doesn't mean they will find true love together. Another well complemented type for INFPs are ENFJs.

The one incompatibility that I've noticed time and time again is between Intuitives (N's) and Sensors (S's). I think this is because these two groups have fundamentally different ways of interacting with the world and often have trouble understanding one another.

In my own experience in romantic relationships, friendships, and business partnerships, I (a strong Intuitive - ENFP) have always run into trouble with those who rate highly on the Sensor mode of being.

Beyond that, it's all up in the air. Generally, for organization sake, I would suggest that P's match with a J. The P will benefit from the J's structure and organization, and the J will benefit from the P's creativity and spontaneity.

TIPS FOR DATING AS AN INFP

1. Make a strong effort to express your feelings. Your "default" way of dating may be quite different from what your partner is used to, so make an effort to explain how you feel and why you behave the way you do (or just tell them to read this book).
2. Avoid dating those with a low emotional intelligence. You are very sensitive to criticism and conflict and need someone who can understand you and create a harmonious relationship.
3. INFPs have a strong dislike of conflict, criticism, and confrontation. You will benefit from developing your ability to handle conflict. The only way to do this is with baby steps, one awkward conversation at a time.
4. You may have a tendency to idealize people, or get lost in your own imagination. Just remember that everyone is human, and no partner or relationship will be perfect, so don't be too hard on your partner, or yourself.

TIPS FOR DATING AN INFP

INFPs are interesting, affectionate, caring, and loving partners. With an INFP you will never be bored of the conversation and you'll have the potential to build something truly special. If you learn to work with their "weaknesses," you may find yourself in a very happy and fulfilling relationship.

1. If you find yourself dating an immature INFP, be prepared for disagreements around "reality," as they may skew the facts to fit their own view of the world. This can be especially challenging since conflict or arguments around these "facts"

will likely upset them.

2. INFPs are highly intuitive and will see through most BS. If you're not honest and authentic, they will notice and you'll lose their respect.

3. INFPs have trouble expressing their feelings. Try and help them along by providing opportunities to casually discuss feelings or situations without judgment. Show them you care and that you're genuinely interested in their happiness.

4. INFPs have good communication skills but they also have a strong dislike of conflict, criticism, and confrontation. As their partner, you need to be aware of this and may need to initiate any difficult conversations and encourage the INFP to open up and share how they really feel. During these conversations, go out of your way to be especially gentle and help them through.

5. Once they open up to you, INFPs can be very fun, spontaneous, and adventurous. Embrace this form of expression and enjoy the adventures that follow.

6. INFPs are not organized, keen on schedules, or otherwise interested in repetitive or mundane work. If you want to build a life with an INFP, you must accept this and accept them. Develop systems, hire help, or take responsibility for the details of your life together.

To learn more about how all the types relate and interact, download the free compatibility chart at:

www.PersonalityTypesTraining.com/thrive

IMPROVING YOUR SOCIAL SKILLS

SOCIAL SKILLS TRAINING AND ADVICE ON SOCIAL SITUATIONS

In our always-on, always-connected society of email, text messaging, and, well, anything but face-to-face conversation, social situations can be a challenge for everyone. We merely do not have as many opportunities to practice conversation as we used to.

As introverts, INFPs enjoy time alone and are around others even less than their extrovert counterparts. This means even less time for the natural practice and development of social skills.

Does this mean introverts are doomed to a life of awkward interactions and social anxiety? Absolutely not. In fact, it is quite the contrary.

When they invest time into developing their social skills, introverts can become just as capable in social situations as extroverts. This gives them a well-rounded personality and an excellent advantage: the ability to chat and socialize when they want, and to sit quietly and listen to others when the situation calls for it. No one likes the person who always has to be the center of attention, right?

This chapter is broken into seven sections, each covering a particular social skill or kind of social situation. At the end of the chapter, you will find a list of additional resources to help you continue working on your social skills.

BEING INTERESTED

I have heard it said that being interested in others is the fastest route to becoming the most interesting person in the room. Show a genuine interest in others and you will be well liked.

When you take an interest in another person, a few powerful things happen.

1 - You build rapport and the other person starts to like you.

2 - You learn important details about the other person. You can then use these details to create conversation around common interests.

When learning about another person, what you ask is almost as important as how you ask it. Typical small talk questions like "So what do you do?" are as boring as they are uninformative. Try using some of the questions below and you will find yourself in much more stimulating conversations.

- What is your biggest goal for this year?
  (Can be followed up by: Why? What challenges do you see coming up?)
- What is your favorite part about your career/hobby/relationship/hometown?
- What is the biggest challenge you are currently facing in your work/school/life?
- I have noticed that you are really good at (insert something you have noticed - for example their style, conversation, telling jokes, business, or cooking). What is your secret? Could you share two or three tips for an amateur like me?

When you are asking questions about their goals or challenges, you are giving yourself an opportunity to offer advice or help them find a solution. You will be amazed at how far this can go, and how much more stimulating the conversation can become when you are working on solving a problem.

In terms of how you approach this, just be curious and thoughtful in your mindset and you will do just fine.

GETTING OUTSIDE OF YOURSELF

The curious thing is that most people at social events are all thinking the same thing: "I wonder what other people are thinking about me."

When you come to realize and truly accept this, everything changes. If you are friendly and kind, you will be amazed at how many people will be drawn to you (especially other introverts!).

Of course, much of our anxiety in social situations goes back to the same question playing in our heads: "I wonder what others are thinking about me."

How do you get past this? Look no further than the last tip: Be genuinely interested in other people. When you move your focus to understanding and caring about others, it is almost impossible to focus on yourself at the same time.

SAY SOMETHING PLEASANT

One compliment can, and will, change someone's whole night.

So, why don't we give people more compliments? One reason is that we get stuck in our heads, wondering what to say and how to say it. We worry about coming off as inauthentic, offending someone, or appearing like a kiss ass. We wonder whether our compliment could be misinterpreted or get us into an awkward situation. Although all these fears are normal, they are also all unfounded.

The key to giving an excellent compliment is in the details, so pay attention to them. Some people spend hours picking out their outfits - nothing is left to chance. Sometimes there will be an obvious "point of pride," such as a new dress or piece of jewelry the person is just waiting to be complimented on. Other times it might not be so obvious, so try these tips:

- For a man, his watch or tie is always a safe compliment (from a man or a woman). From a woman to a man, well, you can get away with complimenting anything.
- For women, jewelry, purses, and shoes are always a point of pride and a safe compliment from another woman.

For the guys, it is a little more complicated. If you don't know the woman well, keep it casual in what you compliment and how you say it. Fashionable jewelry, a trendy phone case, or a colorful watch are safe bets and good conversation starters. Follow up your compliment by asking where they got it, or if there is a groovy story behind it. For example: "That's a really cool watch. Is there a story behind it?"

If you already know the woman, a new hairstyle or piece of clothing is also begging for your compliment.

- Always be as authentic as possible. Look for something you do like in someone, whether it is something physical or a character trait. You will never upset someone by mentioning their excellent sense of humor.
- Sometimes you will be able to notice an area someone is trying to improve and is perhaps self-conscious about. For instance, you may notice a fellow introvert making a big effort to be social and telling a story to a group of people. This is an amazing opportunity...use it.

It's not hard to say, "That was really funny, you know. You are a wonderful storyteller." Yet a few kind words on your part here could make an unforgettable impact and go a long way in building their confidence and encouraging them to continue growing. In doing so, not only do you make someone else feel great, you also make them feel good about you.

PLEASE AND THANK YOU

One of the challenges many introvert types face is a dislike of doing things "just because," particularly when it comes to social norms and etiquette. To the outside world it can appear as rude or inconsiderate when an INFP does not say thank you to their host for having them over for dinner. In reality, the INFP may be very appreciative, they just don't see the need for pleasantries (or they just forgot). They may also take it for granted, assuming the other person knows how much they care about them, or assuming a close friend does not need to be thanked.

The problem is that some people are overly sensitive or just stuck in their ways. Sometimes a lack of "etiquette" can cause unnecessary hostility or conflict, especially with those who do not know you as well, such as a good friend's spouse.

Two things you can do:

Option 1: Make an effort to build habits around manners and etiquette. Perhaps it does not make sense to thank someone for passing the salt, but just do it anyway.

Option 2: Take a few minutes to speak to, or write a note to, the most important people in your life. Tell them how much you value your relationship and explain to them that social norms are not exactly your thing. Make it clear how much you value them and everything they do for you, even if you do not express it at the moment they do it.

Once a year, say around Christmas, send out handwritten cards to your closest friends and make sure to include a note about how much you appreciate them and how happy you are that they are part of your life.

If you do these two things, not only will they not care when you forget a "thank you," you will stand out as one of the most caring and thoughtful people they know.

Explaining Nerves and Social Anxiety

As we walked into one of our regular cafés, my girlfriend reminded me to say hi to her friend working there. "She was upset that you did not say goodbye last time."

This sparked a conversation on "hi and bye" etiquette, and approaching people working or in a group. I explained that most of the time when someone does not come over and say hi they are not trying to be rude. Usually there is something else going on. Often this something else is nervousness or social anxiety. Approaching a group of people to say hello when you only know one or two of them can cause much stress. Logically it probably should not, but alas, it does. One option is to face the nerves and awkwardly approach the group, then stand there waiting to be invited to sit or for the right time to walk away. The other option is a brief wave, or to pretend you did not see them and move on. In this case, you risk being considered rude, or having people think you do not like them, or are mad at them.

Isn't it funny, the wide gap between two people's perceptions?

Unfortunately, there is no magic cure for this situation, although, for the sake of personal growth, I would encourage you to try to say hello whenever possible.

Although there is no magic cure, there is a way you can limit the potential damage (and possibly make the situation a lot easier in the future).

The solution is along the same lines as the one in the "Please and Thank You" section. You need to initiate an honest discussion with friends. For an extreme introvert, the idea of being nervous about approaching a group of people is almost confusing. To them, the only possible explanation is rudeness or a disinterest in them.

Yet guess what happens when you explain the situation from your point of view? They start to understand. Not only will they "get it" when you do not approach them within a group, they may even spot you and come to say hello to you first.

Note: In this section, I use the term social anxiety to describe nervousness or anxiety, around situations. If the negative emotions are so strong that they negatively influence your life, or the anxiety is constant, we may be talking about a more serious form of social anxiety. If this sounds like you, I encourage you to read: Self Confidence Secrets: How To Overcome Anxiety, Fear, and Low Self-Esteem With NLP.

I have received many emails from readers telling me that this book has helped them overcome (sometimes crippling) social anxiety and build their confidence.

Find it on Amazon.com

AVOID CRITICIZING AND COMPLAINING

You are at a social event and you feel uncomfortable. You didn't really want to go in the first place, and now you are dreading your decision to "give it a try." You find yourself at the bar when a fellow guest, equally disappointed, strikes up a conversation with you:

"Why are these things always so boring? This might be the

worst one yet."

Now it is your turn to speak. How do you respond?

It is easy to fall into this negativity trap. Being critical of others is one of the easiest ways to feel better about yourself (in the moment) and temporarily bond with others. The problem is that it's a short-term solution with many negative long-term consequences. Complaining and criticizing brings you down emotionally, eliminates any drive to become more social, and almost guarantees the night will not get any better.

What is more? When you become a complainer, you repel the people you would have the most fun talking with and the ones who are likely in charge of deciding who will get invited back.

Sure, in that moment, never being invited back may sound like a blessing. Would it not be better to get invited back and just decline the invitation if you do not want to go?

ESCAPING THE SMALL TALK TRAP: DIRECT THE CONVERSATION, ASK QUESTIONS, AND GET HELP

Nothing is worse than the *Small Talk Trap*. You are at a social event where you hardly know anyone and find yourself in a conversation with a stranger. Initially the conversation provides relief from the awkward agony of "working the room," but soon the conversation is just as painful. You find yourself thinking back to biology class wondering how much long-term damage would come from jumping out the second story window behind you and making a run for it.

It doesn't have to be like this! There is a better way.

Here are three skills you can use to make your conversations more stimulating.

Strategy #1 - Direct It. There is a good chance the other person does not want to talk about the weather any more than you do. Even if they do, why leave it up to them?

When you go to an event, have a few thought-provoking conversation topics in mind. Ideally, these should be interesting to you and the kind of people you like to talk with. An example could be a book you just read about another culture or a philosophy you have been studying. When the weather comes up for the third time in a conversation, it is time to change it with this simple phrase:

"Hey, sorry to interrupt, but I would love your opinion on something before I forget. I have been reading this book on Stoic philosophy and it has been bombarding me with ideas about how to live life. I keep wondering how these ideas can relate to our modern lifestyle. Do you know much about Stoicism?"

At this point they might be familiar with the topic. That's excellent. If they are not, it is a chance for you to explain it to them. In doing so, you will crystalize your knowledge of the topic and hopefully teach them something interesting in the process.

Sure, some will not have a lot to say, but others will. Either way, you will have a much better time in this conversation than one about weather or sports!

Strategy #2 - Ask Questions. Most people have at least one worthwhile trait or area of knowledge. If you find yourself trapped in a painful conversation, use it as your chance to learn something new.

Start by asking a few quick background questions about the person's home country, work, and hobbies. From there you will be able to find something thought-provoking to zero in on and learn more about. Are they from a far-off country you have always wanted to know more about? Turn this into an opportunity to learn a few phrases in a new language, to discover a few cultural differences, or ask about possible economic opportunities.

Perhaps they study a martial art you have always wanted to learn. You could ask them for advice on the best way to get started, and then how to spend your time in this activity for the first three months.

It won't always be the most fascinating conversation you've ever had, but it's still better than typical small talk.

Strategy #3 - Get Help. This one can be trickier, but once mastered, is a ninja skill of social situations. If you are speaking one-on-one with someone and the conversation is leaving a lot to be desired, try to bring in another person.

The easiest way to do this is when you spot someone you know, or a stranger standing alone, and just motion for them to join you. If this is not an option, there is always Plan B. Take the conversation to a point where you need an opinion on something. Perhaps you decide to disagree on what city has the best weather, or which appetizer at the party is best. Whatever it is, use it as an opportunity to seek another opinion from someone walking or standing nearby: "Excuse me, we were just debating this and would love another opinion. What do you think...?"

However you do it, two things can happen when you bring in a new person:

One, they could be a stimulating conversationalist and change your night for the better. Often, when this happens, your original conversation partner will eventually excuse themselves and you will be left with an enjoyable conversation and possibly a new friend. If the conversation does not improve, at least you have given yourself a less awkward escape route because you will not be leaving anyone alone.

Another upside of this approach is that you may be saving someone else from the awkwardness of standing alone, and they will be grateful for it.

ADDITIONAL RESOURCES ON SOCIAL SKILLS

If you enjoyed this section and want to continue your study of people and social skills, here are a few books to get you started.

- Networking for People Who Hate Networking: A Field Guide for Introverts, the Overwhelmed, and the Underconnected
- Self-Promotion for Introverts: The Quiet Guide to Getting Ahead
- The Introverted Leader: Building on Your Quiet Strength
- Quiet: The Power of Introverts in a World That Can't Stop Talking
- Quiet Influence: The Introvert's Guide to Making a Difference
- The Introvert Advantage: Making the Most of Your Inner Strengths

QUOTES TO MAKE AN INFP SMILE

To end with, I've included a collection of fun, inspiring, and relatable quotes for INFPs. Many are from INFPs, others are simply enjoyable for INFPs.

> *"People understand me so poorly that they don't even understand my complaint about them not understanding me."*
>
> **-SOREN KIERKEGAARD**

> *"In the depth of winter, I finally learned that within me there lay an invincible summer."*
>
> **-ALBERT CAMUS**

> *"Nobody realizes that some people expend tremendous energy merely to be normal."*
>
> **-ALBERT CAMUS**

> *"I'm tired of feeling like I'm fucking crazy."*
>
> **-LANA DEL REY**

"I came to terms with not fitting in a long time ago. I never really fitted in. I don't want to fit in. And now people are buying into that."

-ALEXANDER MCQUEEN

"The future belongs to those who believe in the beauty of their dreams."

-ELEANOR ROOSEVELT

"I was born with an enormous need for affection, and a terrible need to give it."

-AUDREY HEPBURN

"There is something sinister, something quite biographical about what I do - but that part is for me. It's my personal business. I think there is a lot of romance, melancholy. There's a sadness to it, but there's romance in sadness. I suppose I am a very melancholy person."

-ALEXANDER MCQUEEN

✓ *"I can't think of any greater happiness than to be with you all the time, without interruption, endlessly, even though I feel that here in this world there's no undisturbed place for our love, neither in the village nor anywhere else; and I dream of a grave, deep and narrow, where we could clasp each other in our arms as with clamps, and I would hide my face in you and you would hide your face in me, and nobody would ever see us anymore."*

-FRANZ KAFKA

"Weekends don't count unless you spend them doing something completely pointless."

-BILL WATTERSON

"The reward for conformity is that everyone likes you but yourself."

-RITA MAE BROWN

"A person starts dying when they stop dreaming."

-BRIAN WILLIAMS

"People find my things sometimes aggressive. But I don't see it as aggressive. I see it as romantic, dealing with a dark side of personality."

-ALEXANDER MCQUEEN

"To be one's self, and unafraid whether right or wrong, is more admirable than the easy cowardice of surrender to conformity."

-IRVING WALLACE

"You do not need to leave your room. Remain sitting at your table and listen. Do not even listen, simply wait, be quiet, still and solitary. The world will freely offer itself to you to be unmasked, it has no choice, it will roll in ecstasy at your feet."

-FRANZ KAFKA

"He has not learned the first lesson of life who does not every day surmount a fear."

-JOHN DRYDEN

"Your task is not to seek for love, but merely to seek and find all the barriers within yourself that you have built against it."

-RUMI

"The only journey is the one within."

-RAINER MARIA RILKE

"I love being alone, but find my loneliness uncomfortable."

-EGUIZEEY (REDDITOR)

"I believe one writes because one has to create a world in which one can live. I could not live in any of the worlds offered to me — the world of my parents, the world of war, the world of politics. I had to create a world of my own, like a climate, a country, an atmosphere in which I could breathe, reign, and recreate myself when destroyed by living."

-ANAIS NIN

"You must have chaos within you to give birth to a dancing star."

-FRIEDRICH NIETZSCHE

"I like too many things and get all confused and hung-up running from one falling star to another till I drop. This is the night, what it does to you. I had nothing to offer anybody except my own confusion."

-JACK KEROUAC

✓ *"Not all those who wander are lost."*

-J.R.R. TOLKIEN

"Either I'm a genius or I'm mad, which is it? "No," I said, "I can't be mad because nobody's put me away; therefore I'm a genius." Genius is a form of madness and we're all that way. But I used to be coy about it, like me guitar playing. But if there's such a thing as genius — I am one. And if there isn't, I don't care."

-JOHN LENNON

✓ *"When you're an introvert like me and you've been lonely for a while, and then you find someone who understands you, you become really attached to them. It's a real release."*

-LANA DEL REY

"No one respects a talent that is concealed."

-DESIDERIUS ERASMUS

"The individual has always had to struggle to keep from being overwhelmed by the tribe. To be your own man is a hard business. If you try it, you'll be lonely often, and sometimes frightened. But no price is too high to pay for the privilege of owning yourself."

-RUDYARD KIPLING

"It's always better to leave the party early."

-BILL WATTERSON

"There can't be any large-scale revolution until there's a personal revolution, on an individual level. It's got to happen inside first."

-JIM MORRISON

"The mind is its own place and in itself, can make a Heaven of Hell, a Hell of Heaven."

-JOHN MILTON

✓ "If you think that happiness means total peace, you will never be happy. Peace comes from the acceptance of the part of you that can never be at peace. It will always be in conflict. If you accept that, everything gets a lot better."

-JOSS WHEDON

"When others demand that we become the people they want us to be, they force us to destroy the person we really are. It's a subtle kind of murder ... the most loving parents and relatives commit this murder with smiles on their faces."

-JIM MORRISON

"If you only read the books that everyone else is reading, you can only think what everyone else is thinking."

-HARUKI MURAKAMI

"Use loneliness. Its ache creates urgency to reconnect with the world. Take that aching and use it to propel you deeper into your need for expression – to speak, to say who you are."

-NATALIE GOLDBERG

"The most exhausting effort in my life has been to suppress my own nature in order to make it serve my biggest plans."

-ALBERT CAMUS

"You cannot find peace by avoiding life."

-VIRGINIA WOOLF

✓ *"When it is dark enough, you can see the stars."*

-RALPH WALDO EMERSON

"*Believing that you can move mountains sometimes is more important than actually having the ability to do so.*"

-JOSHUA KUSHNER

"*I read a book one day and my whole life was changed.*"

-ORHAN PAMUK

"*The most painful thing is losing yourself in the process of loving someone too much, and forgetting that you are special too.*"

-ERNEST HEMINGWAY

"*I love sleep. My life has the tendency to fall apart when I'm awake, you know?*"

-ERNEST HEMINGWAY

"Don't ever mistake my silence for ignorance, my calmness for acceptance, or my kindness for weakness."

-ANONYMOUS

"Something is always born of excess: great art was born of great terrors, great loneliness, great inhibitions, instabilities, and it always balances them."

-ANAIS NIN

"I find beauty in melancholy."

-ALEXANDER MCQUEEN

"Who are you? Are you in touch with all of your darkest fantasies? Have you created a life for yourself where you can experience them? I have. I am fucking crazy. But I am free."

-LANA DEL REY

"For years I've wanted to live according to everyone else's morals. I've forced myself to live like everyone else, to look like everyone else. I said what was necessary to join together, even when I felt separate. And after all of this, catastrophe came. Now I wander amid the debris, I am lawless, torn to pieces, alone and accepting to be so, resigned to my singularity and to my infirmities. And I must rebuild a truth–after having lived all my life in a sort of lie."

-ALBERT CAMUS

"All my life I've felt like the largest outcast, driven by an unquestioning need to belong and to conform. I still feel it now. But I'm close to the point of not caring."

-MICHELLE LARA LIN

"That is part of the beauty of all literature. You discover that your longings are universal longings, that you're not lonely and isolated from anyone. You belong."

-F. SCOTT FITZGERALD

"Imagination is not only the uniquely human capacity to envision that which is not, and therefore the fount of all invention and innovation. In its arguably most transformative and revelatory capacity, it is the power to that enables us to empathize with humans whose experiences we have never shared."

-J.K. ROWLING

"If you do not tell the truth about yourself you cannot tell it about other people."

-VIRGINIA WOOLF

"Surround yourself with the dreamers and the doers, the believers and the thinkers, but most of all, surround yourself with those who see the greatness within you, even when you don't see it yourself."

-EDMUND LEE

"You can't try and find love. You must let it come to you. As all things good, they must ensue."

-ADRIEL LIM

"I wish they would only take me as I am."

-VINCENT VAN GOGH

"We don't devote enough scientific research to finding a cure for jerks."

-BILL WATTERSON

"Yes: I am a dreamer. For a dreamer is one who can only find his way by moonlight, and his punishment is that he sees the dawn before the rest of the world."

-GILBERT

KEYS TO WEALTH, HEALTH, HAPPINESS, AND SUCCESS

I hope this book has provided some insights into how you can succeed in the most important areas of your life.

In this last section I'd like to share eleven strategies for finding all around success. These strategies will help you enjoy more wealth, health, and happiness in your life.

1. INFPs must follow their passions and do work they love. When interested in something, INFPs have an intense energy and enthusiasm. When stuck doing work they don't enjoy, INFPs are masters of procrastination and excuses.

2. INFPs really dislike repetitive work, so stick to "project based" work or work with people, as that is always a little varied.

3. Look out for your own needs. Your concern for those around you is a wonderful trait, but there will come times where you must step aside and take care of yourself. Sometimes this will mean letting others down, that's OK. People will understand.

4. Develop your External Intuition - your ability to objectively perceive and understand the outside world. This will help you take in all the information and form more accurate perceptions of the people and world around you.

5. Develop your "T" quality. Make a conscious effort to understand and become aware of your emotions, and apply logic to your decision making. This will allow you

to become more objective and disciplined. One way to do this is to learn from the NTs in your life, particularly the INTJs and ENTJs.

6. Take time to compare your initial dreams, goals, or visions with what actually did happen. INFPs have a wonderfully optimistic outlook on life. Unfortunately they also excel at setting "pie in the sky" goals with unrealistic timeframes, and, as such, never actually achieve anything. Developing an accurate perception of how long things really take will help you set and achieve goals and make real progress.

7. On the note of perception, INFPs can sometimes be too hard on other people and have unrealistic expectations for what relationships should be like. Fuelled by movies and Usher songs, INFPs can be quick to skip town the moment their partner reveals a flaw or when a challenge presents itself in the relationship. INFPs will be well served to sit back and OBJECTIVELY look at themselves. Perhaps they will discover they're not perfect either. You may want to enroll a friend or former partner for help in this process.

8. Similar to #7, INFPs are often far too hard on themselves. You have very high standards for yourself and that's good, but comparing yourself to your lofty (often unrealistic) vision can lead to unfair judgments and self-destructive thinking. Take time to review your accomplishments, progress, and positive traits. Don't be afraid to express these thoughts to others around you and allow them to flatter you with kind words.

9. INFPs have a distain for conflict, confrontation, and

being told what to do. In the real world, there will be times when you need to be in these kinds of situations. When negative emotions come up, take a moment to understand them - for example, "I'm feeling upset and I think it is because I am being told what to do."

Then think through the situation and take the most productive and mature action you can.

10. Face your fears to overcome your weaknesses. Learn to express your opinions in the face of criticism, be decisive, and be OK with confrontation. This will only happen by taking action, which at first could be very uncomfortable. Over time, you will develop this muscle and it will get easier and easier.

11. Learn to understand others. You have a unique and wonderful way of looking at the world...but it is one of many and is no more right than any others. Learn to understand how other people see the world, and your influence will increase while the amount of conflict in your world decreases.

PRACTICAL SOLUTIONS TO COMMON CHALLENGES

There is an old-fashioned attitude that tells us to just tough it up, overcome our weaknesses, and do everything ourselves.

This is stupid.

If you're an exceptional painter you should spend your time painting and leave the toilet cleaning to someone else.

The more you allow yourself to offload the tasks and responsibilities you don't enjoy, the more success you will experience. Here are a few practical ideas for making the most of your strengths while avoiding your weaknesses.

Hire Help With:

- Accounting
- Cleaning
- Laundry
- Planning travel
- Organization
- Scheduling
- Life planning (such as a coach)
- Business planning

NEXT STEPS

To help you get the most from this book, I have created a collection of free extras to support you along the way. If you haven't already done so, take a few minutes now to request the free bonuses; you already paid for them when you bought this book. To download these, simply visit the special section of my website: www.PersonalityTypesTraining.com/thrive

There, you will be asked to enter your email address so I can send you the "Thriving Bonus Pack." You'll receive:

- A 5-part mini-course (delivered via email) with tips on how to adjust your life so that you can best make use of your strengths.
- A compatibility chart showing how you are most likely to relate to the other 15 personality types. You'll discover which types are most compatible with you and which types will likely lead to headaches.
- A PDF workbook that complements this book. It's formatted to be printed, so you can fill in your answers to the exercises in each chapter as you go.

To download the Thriving Bonus Pack, visit:

www.PersonalityTypesTraining.com/thrive

SUGGESTIONS AND FEEDBACK

Like the field of psychology, this book will always be growing and improving.

If there's something about this book you didn't like, or there is a point you disagreed with, I'd love to hear from you. Perhaps I missed something in my research.

As well, if you're an "experienced" INFP and you'd like to add your personal story, insight, wisdom, or advice to upcoming editions, my readers and I would love to hear from you.

To contribute in any way, you can email me at: me@thedanjohnston.com.

A SMALL FAVOR

If you've enjoyed this book or found it useful, I'd be very grateful if you'd post a short review on Amazon. Your support really does make a difference, and I read all the reviews personally so I can get your feedback and make this book even better.

If you'd like to leave a review, then all you need to do is visit this book's page on Amazon.

Thanks again for your support!

OTHER BOOKS ABOUT INFPS AND THEIR MOST COMPATIBLE TYPES: ENTJS AND ENFJS

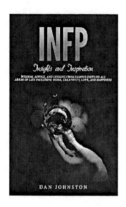

INFP: Insights and Inspiration

Or just visit Amazon and search for "INFP". Then look for the book by Dan Johnston.

ENTJ: The Unstoppable Fieldmarshal and Executive

Or just visit Amazon and search for "ENTJ". Then look for the book by Dan Johnston.

ENTJ: Wisdom from the Top

Or just visit Amazon and search for "ENTJ". Then look for the book by Dan Johnston.

ENFJ: The Leader, Teacher, and People Person

Or just visit Amazon and search for "ENFJ". Then look for the book by Dan Johnston.

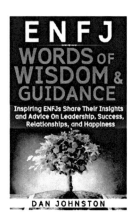

ENFJ: Words of Wisdom and Guidance

Or just visit Amazon and search for "ENFJ". Then look for the book by Dan Johnston..

BOOKS IN THE THRIVE PERSONALITY TYPE SERIES

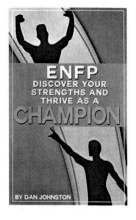

ENFP: The Inspiring Champion

Or just visit Amazon and search for "ENFP". Then look for the book by Dan Johnston.

INFJ: The Protector and Most Disciplined Of Idealists

Or just visit Amazon and search for "INFJ". Then look for the book by Dan Johnston.

INTJ: The Persistent and Strategic Mastermind

Or just visit Amazon and search for "INTJ". Then look for the book by Dan Johnston.

ENTP: The Charming and Visionary Inventor

Or just visit Amazon and search for "ENTP". Then look for the book by Dan Johnston.

INTP: The Often Genius Thinker and Architect

Or just visit Amazon and search for "INTP". Then look for the book by Dan Johnston.

THRIVE SERIES COLLECTIONS

The Idealists: Learning To Thrive As, and With, ENFPs, INFPs, ENFJs, and INFJs

A Collection of Four Books from the Thrive Series.

The Rationals: Learning To Thrive As, and With, The INTJ, ENTJ, INTP, and ENTP Personality Types

A Collection of Four Books from the Thrive Series.

ABOUT THE AUTHOR

Dan Johnston is a #1 international best-selling author, speaker, coach, and recognized expert in the fields of confidence, psychology, and personal transformation. As a coach, one of his specialties is helping clients discover their natural talents, apply them to their true purpose, and create a plan of action to live the life of their dreams.

Dan has been a student of psychology, personal change, and social interaction for over a decade. His passion for helping others feel and be their best drives his continuous pursuit to understand exactly how people work.

Dan's educational background includes a degree in Psychology from a world-renowned university, training with Anthony Robbins at his Leadership Academy, and NLP Practitioner Training with Harry Nichols.

In his personal life, Dan has turned his dreams into reality. Between 2012 and 2013 he lived in five new places: Costa Rica, New York, Germany, Italy, and Spain. Today Dan calls Germany his home base but insists that "home" is wherever he hangs his hat for the week. He frequently travels throughout Europe. Dan spends his mornings writing new books and his early evenings on Skype working one-on-one with his coaching clients, supporting them in creating their own dream lives.

To learn more about Dan Johnston, or inquire about life and business coaching with him, please visit:

www.DreamsAroundTheWorld.com/coaching

For free articles, interviews, and resources on entrepreneurship, pursuing your passions, travel, and creating the life of your dreams, visit Dreams Around The World and subscribe to the "Business Takeoff Training":

www.DreamsAroundTheWorld.com

Find more books by Dan Johnston on his Amazon Author Central Pages:

Amazon.com:

http://www.amazon.com/author/danjohnston

Amazon.co.uk:

http://www.amazon.co.uk/-/e/B00E1DO6OS

CPSIA information can be obtained at www.ICGtesting.com
Printed in the USA
LVOW10s2314040416

482112LV00034B/1055/P